Life-Changing Lessons

PSALMS
VOLUME 2

New Community Bible Study Series

BILL HYBELS

WITH KEVIN & SHERRY HARNEY

New Community

KNOWING. LOVING. SERVING. CELEBRATING.

Life-Changing
Lessons

PSALMS
VOLUME 2

 ZONDERVAN®

 WILLOW
Willow Creek Resources

ZONDERVAN.com/
AUTHORTRACKER
follow your favorite authors

ZONDERVAN®

Psalms Volume 2: Life-Changing Lessons
Copyright © 2008 by Willow Creek Association

Requests for information should be addressed to:

Zondervan, *Grand Rapids, Michigan* 49530

ISBN 978-0-310-28048-4

Interior design by Sherri Hoffman

Printed in the United States of America

08 09 10 11 12 13 14 • 21 20 19 18 17 16 15 14 13 12 11 10 9 8 7 6 5 4 3 2 1

CONTENTS

God has created us for community. This need is built into the very fiber of our being, the DNA of our spirit. As Christians, our deepest desire is to see the truth of God's Word as it influences our relationships with others. We long for a dynamic encounter with God's Word, intimate closeness with his people, and radical transformation of our lives. But how can we accomplish those three difficult tasks?

The New Community Bible Study Series creates a place for all of this to happen. In-depth Bible study, community-building opportunities, and life-changing applications are all built into every session of this small group study guide.

How to Build Community

How do we build a strong, healthy Christian community? The whole concept for this study grows out of a fundamental understanding of Christian community that is dynamic and transformational. We believe that Christians don't simply gather to exchange doctrinal affirmations. Rather, believers are called by God to get into each other's lives. We are family, for better or for worse, and we need to connect with each other.

Community is not built through sitting in the same building and singing the same songs. It is forged in the fires of life. When we know each other deeply—the good, the bad, and the ugly—community is experienced. Community grows when we learn to rejoice with one another, celebrating life. Roots grow deep when we know we are loved by others and are free to extend love to them as well. Finally, community deepens and is built when we commit to serve each other and let others serve us. This process of doing ministry and humbly receiving the ministry of others is critical for healthy community life.

Build Community Through Knowing and Being Known

We all long to know others deeply and to be fully known by them. Although we might run from this level of intimacy at times, we all want to have people in our lives who trust us enough to disclose the deep and tender parts of themselves. In turn, we want to reveal some of our feelings, expressing them freely to people we trust.

The first section of each of these six studies creates a place for deep knowing and being known. Through serious reflection on the truth of Scripture, you will be invited to communicate parts of your heart and life with your small group members. You might even discover yourself opening parts of your heart that you have thus far kept hidden. The Bible study and discussion questions do not encourage surface conversation. The only way to go deep in knowing others and being known by them is to dig deep, and this takes work. Knowing others also takes trust—that you will honor each other and respect each other's confidences.

Build Community Through Celebrating and Being Celebrated

If you have not had a good blush recently, read a short book in the Bible called Song of Songs. It's a record of a bride and groom writing poetic and romantic love letters to each other. They are freely celebrating every conceivable aspect of each other's personality, character, and physical appearance. At one point the groom says, "You have made my heart beat fast with a single glance from your eyes." Song of Songs is a reckless celebration of life, love, and all that is good.

We need to recapture the joy and freedom of celebration. In every session of this study, your group will commit to celebrate together. Although there are many ways to express joy, we will let our expression of celebration come through prayer. In each session you will take time to come before the God of joy and celebrate who he is and what he is doing. You will also have opportunity to celebrate what God is doing in your life and the lives of those who are a part of your small group. You will become a community of affirmation, celebration, and joy through your prayer time together.

You will need to be sensitive during this time of prayer together. Not everyone feels comfortable praying with a group of people. Be aware that each person is starting at a different place in their freedom to pray in a group, so be patient. Seek to promote a warm and welcoming atmosphere where each person can stretch a little and learn what it means to be a community that celebrates with God in the center.

Build Community Through Loving and Being Loved

Unless we are exchanging deeply committed levels of love with a few people, we will die slowly on the inside. This is precisely why so many people feel almost nothing at all. If we don't learn to exchange love with family and friends, we will eventually grow numb and no longer believe love is even a possibility. This is not God's plan. He hungers for us to be loved and to give love to others. As a matter of fact, he wants this for us even more than we want it for ourselves.

Every session in this study will address the area of loving and being loved. You will be challenged, in your personal life and as a small group, to be intentional and consistent about building loving relationships. You will get practical tools and be encouraged to set measurable goals for giving and receiving love.

Build Community Through Serving and Being Served

Community is about serving and humbly allowing others to serve you. The single most stirring example of this is recorded in John 13, where Jesus takes the position of the lowest servant and washes the feet of his followers. He gives them a powerful example and then calls them to follow. Servanthood is at the very core of community. To sustain deep relationships over a long period of time, there must be humility and a willingness to serve each other.

At the close of each session will be a clear challenge to servanthood. As a group, and as individual followers of Christ, you will discover that community is built through serving others. You will also find that your own small group members will grow in their ability to extend service to your life.

Bible Study Basics

To get the most out of this study, you will need to prepare and participate. Here are some guidelines to help you.

Preparing for the Study

1. If possible, even if you are not the leader, look over each session before you meet, read the Bible passages, and answer the questions. The more you are prepared, the more you will gain from the study.
2. Begin your preparation with prayer. Ask God to help you understand the passage and apply it to your life.
3. A good modern translation, such as the New International Version, Today's New International Version, the New American Standard Bible, or the New Revised Standard Version, will give you the most help. Questions in this guide are based on the New International Version.
4. Read and reread the passages. You must know what the passage says before you can understand what it means and how it applies to you.
5. Write your answers in the spaces provided in the study guide. This will help you participate more fully in the discussion and will also help you personalize what you are learning.
6. Keep a Bible dictionary handy to look up unfamiliar words, names, or places.

Participating in the Study

1. Be willing to join in the discussion. The leader of the group will not be lecturing but will encourage people to discuss what they have learned in the passage. Plan to share what God has taught you during your preparation time.
2. Stick to the passages being studied. Base your answers on the verses being discussed rather than on outside authorities such as commentaries or your favorite author or speaker.

3. Try to be sensitive to the other members of the group. Listen attentively when they speak, and be affirming whenever you can. This will encourage more hesistant members of the group to participate.
4. Be careful not to dominate the discussion. By all means participate, but allow others to have equal time.
5. If you are a discussion leader or a participant who wants further insights, you will find additional comments in the Leader's Notes at the back of the book.

Psalms Vol. 2:
Life-Changing Lessons

I have an embarrassing admission to make. Sometimes I talk to myself.

I don't talk out loud, so people don't stare at me or think I'm "a bit off." But I do keep a running dialogue going with myself most of the day. For instance, I discuss and make comments on the way I am handling certain work situations. I might make an important decision, and while I am in the midst of processing the situation and asking someone to carry it out I say, "That was a good decision. That was smoothly handled. Good job, Bill." Or, if the decision I am making feels a little shaky I could find myself saying, "Hold on, Bill; slow down; seek some wisdom on this one."

Sometimes, when I am preparing a message and an idea suddenly snaps into focus I say, "That was brilliant." Other times when I look at my notes I say, "That's a bust. What a bad idea. What was I thinking?"

When I think about it, these inner conversations span the scope of my life. I talk with myself about joys and fears, dreams and regrets, little things and the big stuff. I talk to myself almost all day long. But so do you.

Each of us carries on an internal dialogue about all kinds of subjects. We all talk to ourselves. And, as we grow spiritually and become increasingly aware of the presence of God, we discover that these secret conversations are not really with ourselves as much as with God. And, as we develop meaningful communication with God, we begin to see that much of our life transformation comes as we converse with our Maker in the hidden places of our hearts.

The book of Psalms is really a collection of some secret conversations. One of the reasons I enjoy reading Psalms is that it affords us the rare opportunity to listen in on someone else's private conversation. These are unrehearsed, unpolished, honest, and transparent prayers much like the ones we carry on in our hearts through the day. In many cases, they echo the very topics we pray about. Often the raw emotion that pours through a psalm resonates as we read it because we have felt the same way and have told God so.

In particular, the six psalms featured in this New Community guide express the heart's longing for deep personal transformation. Just like us, the writers of the psalms longed to see God's power unleashed in their lives. They wanted to grow, to be changed, and to see God come alive in every aspect of their lives. So, they talked to God about these things, just like we do.

As you dig into these psalms you might feel like you have opened someone's personal diary and are getting a glimpse into their thoughts, fears, and dreams. That's because you are. But God gives his permission to do so!

The Road to Blessedness

PSALM 1

Some people base their day on a horoscope, hoping the stars will guide them. Others call on a psychic, trying to get some kind of insight into the unknown that lies ahead. All through history people have wanted to get a glimpse over the veil of time and see the future. The truth is that no person can accurately predict events.

Psalm 1 raises a few eyebrows because the psalmist says you can know your future before it happens, that you can be certain of your "blessedness quotient." This psalm contrasts the way of a godly person and the way of the wicked. It claims that certain people are going to experience what the Bible calls "blessedness" in their future.

When you think of this word, *blessedness*, what comes to your mind? Blessedness, as the Bible describes it, is the heart condition the whole world is looking for. It really is. It can't be defined in a short sound bite. But it can be experienced by anyone and everyone who walks through this life with God.

Blessedness is:

- An indescribable inner sense of well-being and total security; a calm assurance of your self-worth
- That vitality of spirit you feel deep down in the core of your being when you know you are rightly related to God and can sense his presence and activity in your life
- The knowledge that you are being conformed into the image of Jesus and being used regularly for his purposes; that your life is making a difference
- The rock-solid confidence and peace that God is providing protection and guidance for your life, that he is in control even in the middle of life's storms and trials

- The certainty that God is going to take you home to be with him someday and that you will spend eternity in his presence

That is blessedness!

Though words can't capture and contain the fullness of biblical blessedness, it is what every heart yearns to experience. And in Psalm 1, God lets us know that we can live in blessedness.

Making the Connection

1. What are some of the ways people try to control their future so that they can feel safe and secure?

Knowing and Being Known

Read Psalm I

2. The psalmist paints a dramatic contrast between the "blessed person" and the "wicked person." What contrasts do you see?

3. Tell about a time in your life that you really experienced biblical blessedness.

What led to this season of intimacy with God and connection to his plan for your life?

Read Psalm 1:1

At the Intersections of Life

The psalmist is painting a picture. You are a traveler along the road of life and you come to a crossroads. As you stop at this intersection, one way points to a call to obedience and following God's plan and teaching; it is the road to blessedness. The other way is also well marked and looks attractive. There are people standing at the intersection calling out to you. Psalm 1 calls them "wicked," "sinners," and "mockers." Like a salesman on commission, they see you and start talking ... they want to sell you their product.

They tell you that the road marked by obedience does not lead to blessedness. They say, "Come on over here; let's have a discussion because you need to know the truth. The road named obedience leads to bondage, narrow-minded living, and it is a moral straitjacket. There is no fulfillment on that road." They offer their counsel, argue their theories, and shout their slogans. "Live for the day!" "You only go around once!" "Nice guys finish last!" "Do unto others before they do unto you!" They will do all they can to get you to follow their counsel and leave the path of blessedness.

4. What are some of the voices in our culture that are shouting out and seeking to get this generation to leave God's road of blessedness and walk the path of the wicked?

What are some examples of how these voices are prevailing and what are some of the consequences?

5. We all hear the voices of the wicked, the sinners, and the mockers. They never shut up! What are some of the things you have done to keep yourself from being distracted and influenced by these voices?

6. Imagine yourself standing at the crossroads and you see a person right there, at the intersection, about to take a step off the road of blessedness and head down the path of the wicked. It all looks and sounds so good. What advice would you give this person?

Read Psalm 1:2; 119:1 – 9; and 2 Timothy 3:14 – 16

Surprising Delight

What do you delight in? We all have things that hit the spot when it comes to personal delight. A comfortable chair, a cold drink, a big bag of chips, Sunday afternoon, a remote control clenched in our fist, and football games on multiple channels. Delight! A roaring fire, a quilt over your knees, a hot cup of coffee, and a good book. Delight! A table covered with food and encircled with family members, great conversations, and hearty laughter. Delight! Each of us has moments in life that bring a depth of emotion that can be described as delight.

The psalmist points out that another way to experience blessedness is to delight in the words of the Bible. He does not say, "Force yourself to read the Bible," or, "Study the Bible because it's good for you." The picture is clear. When we delight in God's teachings and truth revealed in the Bible, we grow in blessedness. As we naturally meditate on the truth of Scripture, day and night, blessing flows. In this life, lots of things can bring us delight, but on the top of the list should be a delight in God's Word.

7. Tell about a person you know who delights in God's Word. How has their example of loving the Bible influenced you?

How does their meditation on the truth of the Bible shape their life and character?

8. How do you seek to grow a love for studying and meditating on the Bible into your life?

9. What is a passage in the Bible that brings you great delight? Read it and share how God speaks to you through it.

If there is a passage in the Bible you have memorized, would you share it with your group and tell them what this portion of Scripture means to you?

An Oasis in a Desert

A blessed person is like a flourishing tree growing by a river. For most of us the picture of a green tree is no big deal. But this psalm was written in a place and time where water was a precious commodity. The image in Psalm 1:3 conveys the idea of an oasis. It is a picture of a tree that is healthy and has an absolutely unlimited supply of water flowing to its roots. There is life, hope, fruitfulness, purpose, and prosperity. What a beautiful picture of what our lives can look like when they draw nourishment, every day, from God!

Read Psalm 1:3; 84:5 – 7; 92:12 – 15; and John 4:13 – 14

10. When you are living in the blessedness of God's presence and drawing life from him, what is some of the fruit that grows in your life?

When you let yourself get disconnected from the flow of his presence and life, how does that affect your fruitfulness?

11. Some people want to define prosperity only in terms of financial gain. When you are walking close with God and drawing from the life of his Spirit, what are some of the ways God allows you to prosper, beyond just dollars and cents?

The Road of Disobedience

All of us face the decision to follow the road of blessedness or the pathway of barrenness on a daily basis. As we grow in community and learn to love each other, we begin to do all we can to help others stay on the right path. The second half of Psalm 1 gives a sobering picture of the cost when we walk the wrong path.

Every time an opportunity arises to make a right choice but we take the wrong path, the psalmist says, prepare for barrenness. It might not come overnight, but it always comes. When we are not planted by the river of God that feeds our souls and lives, a dry season is on the horizon. We will all be tempted by shortcuts that promise immediate profitability, but over the long haul it leads to barrenness. If we continually choose the pathway marked "disobedience" and refuse to listen to the Spirit of God, the Bible warns us that God is not mocked and we will reap what we sow.

Psalm 1 teaches that each of us is going to wind up with great feelings of blessedness or a deep experience of barrenness. It is going to be one or the other. If we want to know which it will be, the psalmist says it is all determined by which road we take at life's most important intersection. The road of obedience leads to blessedness … it's guaranteed. The road of disobedience leads to barrenness. The choice is that clear.

Celebrating and Being Celebrated

We all should learn to notice, drink in, and appreciate moments of blessedness. Then, we should talk about them and celebrate them. In a world filled with bad news, let's learn to rejoice in the great moments of blessedness and delight that take many shapes and forms.

Blessedness in relationships are those unforgettable family joys that come our way. It is when you are at the table, looking around at kids who are laughing and eating and enjoying life; you want to grab your digital camera, take a picture, and put it on your computer screen so you can relive the moment over and over. In these moments you just say, "God, you satisfy my soul. This is a blessed, precious moment."

It is those treasured moments of fellowship with other Christ followers, whether you are meeting over coffee, serving with someone, or just working out together. You are sharing life at a deep and rich level. Your heart cries, "This is a blessed, treasured moment. This is something special that is reserved for God's children."

There are moments of blessedness when there is a miraculous answer to prayer, or a mysterious and yet unmistakable presence of the Holy Spirit. In these moments we say, "This is a precious moment. I am a blessed person."

We all have these moments of profound blessedness, but we don't often share them with others. Take time as a group and tell about a time you experienced the rich blessedness of being God's child. Rejoice and celebrate with each other, and draw hope from each other's stories.

Loving and Being Loved

If you find yourself regularly heading down the road of barrenness, consider asking one of your group members to come alongside and support you in your effort to stay on the path of blessedness. Identify a person whom you trust, who loves God and who loves you. Then, talk with them about the struggles you face and invite them to pray for you, speak into your life, and keep you accountable.

Serving and Being Served

Because reading, knowing, and meditating on God's Word is one of the ways to grow in blessedness and stay on God's path for your life, consider this act of service: If you have children, grandchildren, nieces, nephews, or other young people you can influence, send them a daily email with a short portion or a chapter from the Bible. They might not open the Bible every day, but most of them check their email multiple times each day.

You can get Bible programs for your computer at a reasonable cost and you can even find free Bible programs online. Cut and paste a passage and send it off to the young people in your life. Invite them to read it and share a brief insight with you from the passage (even a sentence or two). This simple act of service can help propel them along on the road to blessedness.

Godly Guilt

PSALM 38

Psalm 38 is about guilt ... godly guilt. There might be some who read these words and say, "All guilt is bad. There is no such thing as godly guilt." But as you dig into Psalm 38, you will see a bigger and clearer picture about the God-honoring place of appropriate guilt.

Any time a group of Christ followers gathers, there will always be a few who are tormented by inappropriate guilt. They feel guilty about almost everything. They hear a message or read a Bible passage about how God wants us to demonstrate compassion for needy people and they begin, almost without thinking, to shoulder the burdens of every person on the planet. They feel guilty that they have a warm meal and a safe home. Even though they are praying, helping, giving, and serving faithfully, they feel great amounts of guilt for not doing more.

Similarly, whenever Christians gather, there will be some who almost never feel any guilt. It is not that these people have gone a long time without sinning. Their lack of guilt exists because they have learned the fine art of denying the existence of their sin. They have developed the art of rationalizing their behavior, excusing their sin, and insulating their hearts from the discomfort of guilt.

Both of these extremes are dangerous. The hypersensitive people who seem to always feel guilty risk the danger of the Evil One whispering, "How could God love somebody like you? How could God ever use you? You will never measure up." These people can become incapacitated by guilt. On the other hand, those who have learned to insulate their hearts from guilt run the risk of developing the disease described in Romans 1:21–32: the ability to keep sinning in the face of a holy God and not even feel bad about it.

There is a healthy and holy middle ground between these two extremes. Godly guilt does not destroy us, but it does break our hearts. It makes us profoundly aware of our sinfulness and our need for grace. Appropriate guilt is a gift from God that helps us turn away from patterns and behaviors that damage us, hurt others, and break the heart of God.

Making the Connection

1. Does your natural disposition tend toward being more sensitive or more thick-skinned?

   How can your natural disposition impact the way you deal with feelings of guilt?

Knowing and Being Known

Read Psalm 38

2. Describe *one* of the following aspects of David's life when he wrote this psalm:

   • David's physical condition

   • David's emotional condition

   • David's relationship with God

   • David's relationship with family and friends

3. What connections does David make between his sin and what he is facing at this time of his life?

Read Psalm 38:1 – 8

Internal Trauma

David's guilt produced internal trauma on many levels. It clearly impacted David's physical and emotional condition. The precious fellowship with God that he so frequently enjoyed is now disrupted and replaced by the fear and the wrath of God. Does this sound like David? David begins the psalm, "O LORD, do not rebuke me in your anger." This is the same man who declared in so many other psalms, "My praise for you shall be continually in my mouth. All I do is think about you and love you." The friendship of God is replaced by the feeling that God is now a foe. David feels the personal, penetrating arrows of the convicting power of God. Guilt has taken its toll. David cries out, "My guilt has overwhelmed me like a burden too heavy to bear."

4. If we keep sin hidden, refuse to confess it, and turn away from it, how might this impact our relationship with God?

5. When we have confessed our sin and seek to repent and turn away from it, how does this impact our relationship with God?

How should this place of humble repentance impact feelings of guilt?

6. Satan loves to lie and deceive, to twist what God wants to do in our lives. What are some of the tactics Satan might try to use on:

   a person who tends to fixate on their own shortcomings and who feels guilty over every little thing

   a person who is great at rationalizing their sin and rarely feels guilty about anything

Relational Trauma

To David, sinning against God was the same as slapping God in the face. Sin to some people is breaking a rule. There is nothing personal or impersonal about it. It is just breaking a religious regulation. If they refuse to love, they broke the rule of love. If they don't tithe, they broke one of the financial laws in Scripture. They tell a lie, another rule broken. But these are just rules. It's like driving a few miles an hour over the speed limit; everyone does it … no big deal!

David never looked at sin that way. To David, sin was a direct insult of the God he loved more than life itself. It was relational betrayal, which is why when he confessed his sin with Bathsheba he said to God, "Against you, you only, have I sinned." David is saying, "Ultimately, I am not breaking rules, I am breaking a relationship with the one who loves me." Sin is relational treason against God.

Read Psalm 38:9–14

7. Some people see sin as simply breaking a rule. Like David, others see sin as "slapping God in the face." How can these two different outlooks on sin influence our choices and actions when we face a temptation?

8. People are fond of saying their choices are "personal" and don't have to do with anyone else. When we commit a sin, even if no one else knows about it, how can this impact the way we relate to family, friends, or other people in our lives?

God's Solution to the Guilt Problem

What is a Christ follower to do when sin comes crashing in? Where does a guilty brother or sister turn when the guilt of sin weighs heavy? When you fall into sin and guilt floods in, don't look at yourself; look up to God. When you are ready to get rid of your guilt, don't look at yourself; you are not the solution. When sin is so present that your body aches and your heart is broken, God is waiting with open arms. He is always ready to forgive.

Religious activity is not the solution to relieving your guilt. Turning over a new leaf, having better intentions—those aren't the solutions to removing guilt. Nor is the answer doing penance, punishing yourself, walking around with your head hanging low.

Sin is an offense against God. This means we must go to God if we want things to be made right. First John 1:9 says, "If we confess our sins, he is faithful and just and will forgive us our sins and purify us from all unrighteousness." God can be trusted. Because of what Jesus did on the cross, because of his sacrifice, we can be cleansed of sin and free of guilt.

Read Psalm 38:15 – 22

9. How do David's tone and perspective change in this final portion of the psalm?

What specific lines of the psalm reveal a changed and hopeful heart?

10. The ultimate plan for guilt removal is simple: confess your sin to God through Jesus Christ. How have you experienced the guilt-banishing freedom of confession?

11. What biblical counsel would you give to a follower of Jesus who says, "I have confessed my sins and accepted Jesus' grace, but I still feel guilty most of the time"?

What biblical counsel would you give to a person who says, "I don't feel the need to confess sin to Jesus or anyone else"?

Celebrating and Being Celebrated

Spend time in prayer as a group thanking God for the grace and forgiveness that have been made available through Jesus. Consider using any of the following passages to inspire you in your prayers:

"Come now, let us reason together,"
    says the LORD.
"Though your sins are like scarlet,
    they shall be as white as snow;
though they are red as crimson,
    they shall be like wool." (Isaiah 1:18)

As far as the east is from the west,
    so far has he removed our transgressions from us.
    (Psalm 103:12)

Because I have sinned against him,
    I will bear the LORD's wrath,
until he pleads my case
    and establishes my right.
He will bring me out into the light;
    I will see his righteousness. (Micah 7:9)

Loving and Being Loved

God gives a beautiful invitation:

Come all you tender hearts, and all you hard hearts. Come to me. Your guilt can be washed away! Come and confess your sinfulness. Look into the face of the One you slapped. Look to me through the death, burial, and resurrection of my Son who paid the price for you. I will set you free. No more stomachaches, no more nausea. The price has been paid. Go and sin no more. Don't put yourself through this. Don't put friends and family through this. Don't put your church through this. Get on with life. Live free from sin and guilt. And, remember, I can still use you. I did great things through Moses after he committed murder. I used Jacob even though he struggled with being deceitful. I led through David after his adultery and murder. I called Peter to lead my church after he denied me three times. I still have a plan for your life. Come and follow me.

Take time on your own and read this invitation. Then, ask God to speak to your heart about how he wants to work in and through your life. If there is anything that needs to be confessed, lay it down. Then give God praise for his grace and new life.

Serving and Being Served

You have learned a great lesson about the freedom from guilt that comes through confession and the finished work of Jesus on the cross. If you know someone who is a follower of Christ but seems to live with chronic guilt, consider meeting with them and sharing what you learned in this session. It will be a gift for them and perhaps God will use your words to help them understand and walk more fully in the grace of Jesus.

Choosing to Trust God

PSALM 56

Have you ever ridden on a spiritual roller coaster? One day you are up, the next you feel down. One moment you are filled to overflowing with faith; the next moment you are crying out, "God, where are you?" One morning you believe that, in God's strength, you can take on the world. But the next morning you don't even feel like getting out of bed.

If you have taken this ride, and most of us have, you probably thought you were the only Christian facing this up-and-down experience. What is surprising is that when you begin to talk honestly with other Christ followers, you discover that this experience is almost universal. All through the Bible there are examples of people who felt deep faith one moment and then faced heart-pounding fear the next. It can look different for each of us, but the up-and-down journey of faith is more common than we think.

Maybe you have mistakenly felt that true Christians have an easy time trusting God. Perhaps you have felt that real Christ followers seldom cave in to worry or fear. You might have thought of yourself as a spiritual oddity because of how often you engage in the battle that rages between faith and fear. Maybe you have even wondered if you are a good Christian because the roller-coaster ride from fear to faith to fear to faith has just plain worn you out. You might even feel a little embarrassed about your roller-coaster faith and don't really want to talk to anyone else about it.

Well, today is honesty time! Some of God's greatest people have faced the same struggle.

Making the Connection

1. Tell about a time you experienced deep faith and confidence in God only to find yourself dealing with fear and a crisis of faith shortly thereafter.

   Why do we tend to avoid talking about how our faith can go up and down like a roller coaster?

   Why is it important that we learn to be honest about these struggles?

Knowing and Being Known

Read Psalm 56

2. What are some of David's expressions of fear, worry, or lament in this psalm?

3. What are some of David's declarations of praise, trust, and confidence in this psalm?

Imagine you are a person who believes that mature Christ followers are always happy, faith-filled, and victorious. How might you view David after reading this psalm?

Welcome to the Real World

Psalm 56 is a written record of a private conversation. It is an unrehearsed, unguarded, off-the-top-of-the-head conversation that David had with God. We might be surprised at what can be gleaned from this rare peek into David's thought life. But if we listen closely and look intently, we can learn and draw some applications to our private conversations with God.

Far too many Christians become discouraged when they have to admit that they drift into fear as often as they do. None of us really wants to put it on the table, turn on the lights, look at it, and talk about it. It is time that all of us hear this simple wake-up call: "Welcome to the real world!" Mature Christ followers still struggle. Godly people deal with fear. Saints face temptations, just like Jesus did. All of us will fight fierce battles of faith. Sometimes we will win and sometimes we will lose. We need to stop berating ourselves for being human. God accepts our humanity and so should we.

Read Psalm 56:1–7

4. Look closely at the first seven verses of this psalm and track David's emotional condition. Write a few words, no more than a sentence, to describe the condition of David's heart in the following passages. Also, indicate if you think David's faith and confidence are heading up or down. When finished, share your descriptions and ratings with the group.

Verses from Psalm 56	Your description of what David is feeling	David's "faith rating" ("up" or "down")
vv. 1–2		
vv. 3–4		
vv. 5–6		
v. 7		

What do you learn about David's walk of faith from these verses?

5. Many Christ followers are fine talking about their faith-filled moments, but are apprehensive talking about times they are filled with fear and their faith quotient is low. What keeps us from being honest and transparent about these faith struggles?

What are some of the benefits we might experience if we would actually talk openly about our struggles, fears, and times of spiritual struggle?

6. If there is an area of your life where you are struggling with fear or your faith is not as strong as you would like it to be, share this with your group members.

How might your group members pray for you and encourage you as you seek to deepen and develop stronger faith in this area of your life?

Choose to Trust

Right in the middle of his fear and struggle, David changes gears. It is as if he says, somewhere deep in his soul, "I will choose to trust in God!" Twice in Psalm 56 David shifts from being fearful to expressing faith-filled and confident words. He decides to trust, even if his circumstances seem painful and hopeless.

There are moments when we need to make the choice to change the channel of our mind. At these times we deliberately choose to trust God no matter what our eyes see or our heart feels. At these times we decide that the best way to live is with confidence, peace, and stability in God. When we make this decision, we reduce the intensity and ups and downs of the roller-coaster ride. We flatten out the hills. But we must know that living trustingly, expectantly, and optimistically requires a conscious choice to trust God.

7. Tell about a time you felt fear and worry invading your heart, but you changed the channel and declared, "I choose to trust in God!" How did this decision and shift in your thinking transform the situation you were facing?

8. If you are facing a time of fear and anxiety in some area of your life (perhaps you shared about it in response to question 6), consider doing *one or more* of the following things:

   • Declare before God, and your group members, that you choose to trust in God as you walk through this experience.
   • Allow your group members to gather around you, lay hands on you, and pray for you to have a fresh, bold, confident faith as you face this situation.
   • Take time with God, one-on-one, each morning to meditate on Psalm 56:4 and to reaffirm that you place your trust in him and will not be paralyzed or controlled by fear.

From the Severity of My Problems to the Sufficiency of God

In order for David to turn the channel of his mind, he had to absolutely focus on the identity and character of God. The more you know about God's character, attributes, and personality, the easier it is to trust in his sufficiency. The clearer you see his track record throughout all of biblical history, church history, your own personal history, the quicker you will be to declare, "In God I trust; I will not be afraid."

This is one of the reasons the people of Israel told stories of God's faithfulness over and over and over again. As we keep reminders of God's presence, character, and past victories on the front burner of our mind, the temperature of our faith increases. Conversely, if we dwell on our problems and focus on our personal weaknesses, our faith cools off. No matter how severe the challenge we face, God's power and presence are always sufficient for us to walk in faith and overcome.

Read Psalm 56:8 – 13

9. In the second half of this psalm, David does not ignore the severity of his situation. Yet he turns his eyes and mind to God. As you study verses 8 – 13, what do you learn about *one* of the following:

    • The real struggles David was facing

    • David's understanding of God's power and character

    • David's hope for the future

10. We grow more confident and faith-filled as we meditate on God's attributes and characteristics. What is an attribute of God that strengthens your faith when you think about it, and how have you experienced this quality in your life?

11. Our faith increases as we tell stories of God's faithfulness in the past. Tell a brief story of how God has been present and powerful in your life, or the life of someone you know and love.

Celebrating and Being Celebrated

God loves you more than you will ever know. He charts every step you take. You have never taken a step, on or off the path, that has gone unnoticed. God has put every tear you have cried in a bottle with your name on it. God is for you.

> The LORD is with me; I will not be afraid.
> What can man do to me? (Psalm 118:6)

> What, then, shall we say in response to this? If God is for us, who can be against us? He who did not spare his own Son, but gave him up for us all—how will he not also, along with him, graciously give us all things? (Romans 8:31–32)

> Then my enemies will turn back when I call for help.
> By this I will know that God is for me. (Psalm 56:9)

Pray as a group and thank God for being on your side. Celebrate all he has done, is doing, and will do to help you walk in faith, no matter what you face in this life.

Loving and Being Loved

The first and greatest commandment is this:

> Jesus replied: "'Love the Lord your God with all your heart and with all your soul and with all your mind.' This is the first and greatest commandment." (Matthew 22:37–38)

If you want to grow in your faith, the best way is to grow in love with God. The more you know of him, the more you can trust him. The more you know of him, the more you can understand who he is. Make time to be with him. Read his Word and find out who he has revealed himself to be. Memorize it and meditate on it. Faith increases as you grow in love with God and get to know him better.

Serving and Being Served

In the course of this session there has been opportunity to be honest and vulnerable. Some of your group members took a risk and shared an area of life where their faith has been waning and they have been struggling. First, serve them by keeping what they have shared within the confines of your group. Second, if one of your group members shared an area of struggle that touched your heart, commit to pray for them and consider encouraging them with a note, email, or phone call this week. Let them know you are praying for them and you are confident that their faith will grow and deepen as they make the decision to trust in God in greater and greater measure.

Fear Not

PSALM 91

A psychologist once said, "There are only two kinds of human beings who are exempt from having to deal with fear: dead people and deranged people." This statement rings true. Every one of us deals with various kinds of fear as we walk through life.

There are the seemingly insignificant concerns of life that we could call *pestering fears*. They don't seem like a big deal, but they take more of a toll on us than we think. Will the Mother's Day dinner turn out right? Will my bonus check cover the cost of the new golf clubs? Will the kids do well on their exams? Will my favorite team win their big game? None of these seems like a big deal. But add up dozens of these and they can start to rock our boat.

We also face situations that are more significant—we might call them *pressing fears*. When these hit, we are more than a little bogged down; the ship starts taking on water. For instance, you hear rumors floating around your workplace that a big company restructure is upcoming and you might lose your job. Or the phone rings and a high school counselor tells you that your child's grades are in a free fall. Or you are in a significant relationship that is filled with tension, with no indication of any resolution on the horizon. These kinds of fears weigh us down, drain our energy, and can even cause mild panic in our hearts.

There is yet another kind of fear that many of us are familiar with, one that can paralyze and immobilize even the strongest of people. We might call this *panic-producing fear*. When someone is diagnosed with a terminal illness (either their own or a loved one's), they can face this level of fear. The same goes for a person who receives a termination notice at work and their vocational and financial worlds turn upside down overnight, or a couple

39

who goes through a divorce, addiction, abuse, or random violence. These life experiences can feel like a gash in the hull of the ship, leaving people bailing out water as fast as they can and feeling like they are fighting a losing battle.

None of us travels far down the road of life without encountering situations that cause fear. Whether pestering fears, pressing fears, or panic-producing fears, the landscape of life will give us ample opportunities to learn how to deal with them.

Making the Connection

1. What is one area of fear you are presently facing? Do you see this as a pestering, pressing, or panic-producing fear?

Knowing and Being Known

Read Psalm 91
2. What are some of the fear-producing situations mentioned in Psalm 91?

How are these similar to what people face today?

3. If a fear-filled person reads this psalm, what statements or truths might bring them hope and alleviate some of their fear?

Recognize Your Refuge

The psalmist begins by letting us know that the best way to overcome any kind of fear, big or small, is to make sure that God is our refuge. If God is truly our shelter, fortress, and refuge, we can make it through anything. In Psalm 91 we meet a man who refuses to fall into fear. In spite of all the apparent chaos and uncertainty around him, though he is tiptoeing through the minefields of life, fear is not dominating him. God is his refuge, and that is always enough.

It would be revealing if we could take a picture with a supernatural camera that would show the stature, the height, of the God we serve. Some serve a knee-high God. Others serve a ceiling-high God; still others, a sky-high God. And there are those who serve the Most High God.

The size of our God is exceedingly important. It is closely connected to whether or not we walk in fear. If we have a knee-high God, there is a lot in life that can overtake and overwhelm us. But if we worship and follow the Most High God, everything looks different.

Read Psalm 91:1 – 2

4. How has God been a refuge and fortress to protect you in the hard times of life?

41

salmist says, "Whoever *dwells* in the shelter of the Most
(Psalm 91:1 TNIV, italics added). There is a sense that
ed to live in his presence. What can we do to dwell
closely in the shelter and presence of God?

Read Psalm 91:3 – 8

Believe God's Promises

It is easy to understand why so many people wander in the wastelands of fear. It is part of being human and living in a fallen world. A natural response to life's uncertainties is fear. Many people feel justified living with a cloud of fear over their heads. They say, "If you live in the real world and realize it is an uncertain place, you will quickly learn that there are good reasons for living in fear." But God wants to invade this kind of thinking and replace it with a bold confidence built on the certainty of his presence, power, and promises.

What God expects, rather, what God commands with respect to fear, is that his children never be controlled by it. The world might excuse a fear-filled life, but God wants to set us free. God says it throughout the Bible. He speaks two powerful words: "Fear not." The apostle Paul writes, "For God did not give us a spirit of timidity, but a spirit of power, of love and of self-discipline" (2 Timothy 1:7). Not only does God *want* us to life a life free from the dominion of fear, he *promises* to help us experience this kind of existence.

6. One of God's greatest promises is that he will be with us; he will not leave or forsake us. How does the promise of God's presence in this psalm and other passages in the Bible bring comfort to those facing fearful circumstances?

Tell about a time you felt the presence of God cover you like wings and describe how this helped to lift your fear.

7. God is all-powerful. He can set captives free, protect us from attacks, bring light in the darkness, heal us from sickness, and perform miracles beyond what we can imagine or dream. Tell about a time you witnessed a work of God that was surprising, supernatural, or miraculous.

Angels Around You

The psalmist says that he refuses to wander in the wastelands of fear because of what angels do. You might say, "You've got to be kidding. We're not really going to start talking about angels in our day and age!" Well, guess what, we don't talk enough about angels. The Bible talks often about the ministry and work of angels, and so should we. This psalm (vv. 11–12) tells us that angels are sent to guard us and lift us up. This is very exciting stuff! Think about it, God has assigned heavenly beings to keep an eye on you and to help you in times of need.

The angel of the LORD encamps around those who fear him,
    and he delivers them. (Psalm 34:7)

"Don't be afraid," the prophet answered. "Those who are with us are more than those who are with them."
And Elisha prayed, "O LORD, open his eyes so he may see." Then the LORD opened the servant's eyes, and he looked and saw the hills full of horses and chariots of fire all around Elisha. (2 Kings 6:16–17)

Are not all angels ministering spirits sent to serve those who will inherit salvation? (Hebrews 1:14)

Read Psalm 91:9 – 13

8. We are told that not only God but angels are watching over us. What are some of the specific supernatural protections this psalm talks about?

If you have experienced a time that you are confident God provided heavenly protection for you, share your story.

Call Out to God

Some Christians tell God their problems over and over again. They get on their knees and pray, but when they are done, they get up and live as unchanged people. They are still fear-filled and paralyzed. This is not the kind of prayer that releases us from the bonds of fear. When we call out to God about a problem, we should remember that he already knows everything about it. We don't need to spend our time repeating the details over and over. As we give God our problems and our fears, we can receive his power, freedom, and boldness to press on. There is power in calling on the name of God. Prayer itself can diffuse fear. This is why the apostle Paul writes, "Do not be anxious about anything, but in everything, by prayer and petition, with thanksgiving, present your requests to God. And the peace of God, which transcends all understanding, will guard your hearts and your minds in Christ Jesus" (Philippians 4:6 – 7).

Read Psalm 91:14 – 16

9. At the end of this psalm, like a crescendo, the call to prayer echoes out. Why is prayer one of the best ways to overcome fear and begin walking in bold confidence?

10. How can your group begin to pray together in deeper and more substantial ways?

Celebrating and Being Celebrated

How tall is your God? How mighty is your God? How tender is your God? How strong is your God? How able is your God? If your God isn't what the God of the Bible reveals himself to be, then your image of him needs adjusting. The God of the Bible, the one true God, is not knee-high, ceiling-high, or even sky-high. He is the Most High God! Take time as a group to lift up prayers celebrating God's power, might, glory, victory over sin, authority over fear, and lordship in your life. If your vision is too small, ask him to expand it.

Loving and Being Loved

Identify a Christ follower you know who lives with a bold and fearless spirit. Take time this week to contact this person and communicate how their example of faith and trust in God has inspired your faith. Thank them for modeling what it looks like to "dwell in the shelter of the Almighty."

Serving and Being Served

Often leaders in the local church come under the attack of the enemy. They can grow weary and discouraged. Take time as a group to pray for your church leaders. Make a brief list of leaders you feel need some spiritual encouragement:

_____

_____

_____

_____

Pray for them to know the bold confidence of living under the shadow of God's wings. Pray, in the name of Jesus, for them to be free from fear and to know the presence of God in new, rich, and life-changing ways.

The Blessings of Obedience

PSALM 112

We live in a generation of extreme sports, X Games, and energy drinks. People are looking for the next big experience, buzz, or high. So they jump out of a plane with a snowboard strapped to their feet, or they free-climb the vertical face of a rock formation, or they try to land a double backflip on a motorcycle. These modern-day thrill seekers make the stunts of Evel Knievel look tame.

You might not do BASE jumping off a skyscraper or ski a glacier, but everyone wants to experience excitement in this life. What do you do to get your adrenaline pumping? What activity in life gets you excited? What do you dream about? What brings the greatest sense of fulfillment and satisfaction?

While the world continues to offer an expanding menu of heart-thumping options, God still leads the best thrill-seeking adventure trips of all. You don't have to go on a safari in Africa or bungee jumping in New Zealand to experience a true rush. All the excitement you could imagine, and more, can be found when you make a decision to obediently follow God's plan for your life. As a matter of fact, the rush, buzz, fulfillment, and satisfaction of a life committed to Jesus Christ bury all the options the world offers.

Making the Connection

1. Tell about an experience you have had that might be considered dangerous, exciting, extreme, or out of the norm (not a spiritual experience, just a heart-thumping life experience).

Read Psalm 112

2. When a person is radically committed to following Jesus, excitement and blessings overflow. Identify one verse in this psalm that connects for you because of the blessing that is promised. What is the blessing and how could it increase the fulfillment level of a person's life?

3. According to this psalm, what are some of the indicators that a person is living a Psalm 112:1 life? (Use the table to record your group responses.)

   Throughout Psalm 112, the psalmist touches on a number of indicators of this kind of life. Most of these indicators are connected with some kind of a statement of what God will do for, in, or with this kind of a person. Take a moment and connect the indicator of obedience to God's response.

Indicator of an obedient life	What God will do for, in, or with this person

Family Blessings

Those who walk obediently with God and are passionate about their faith in Jesus Christ give an amazing gift to the next generation. As God's blessings pour into your life, they just overflow to your children and their children after them. Obedience leads to blessing after blessing that will cascade into future generations. How exciting is this? Each day that we live faithfully as a follower of Jesus, we are investing in those who will come after us.

Practically speaking, how will future generations benefit from your devotion to God? The clearest way this can be illustrated is from a real life. What follows is a snapshot from my own life: I was brought up by godly parents. Almost every day I am aware that I am still receiving the overflow of God's favor upon my dad and mom. The best thing my parents did for me was devote their lives passionately to God, and they did.

Because of their obedience, I grew up in a Christ-centered, loving, and stable home. The very air I breathed under my parents' roof was biblically based and joy filled. What a legacy! Of course, I could not see it or identify it at the time, but there was a flood of blessing pouring into my life, every day, just because I was raised by my parents. I received a heritage that money can't buy. Because of this, God poured into me healthy self-esteem, God-honoring values, an accurate vision of God, and a sense of purpose in this world. As the years pass, I look back and become more and more thankful for the overflow of blessing I have due to the lives of my dad and mom.

Read Psalm 112:1 – 2

4. If you were raised by parents or grandparents who are passionate followers of Jesus, what are some of the family blessings that God allowed to overflow from them to you?

5. If you are a parent, what are some of the blessings you hope and pray will overflow through you to your children's lives?

6. What are some of the things we can do to help God's blessings flow more freely from our lives to the next generation?

Material Blessings

Some preachers and teachers focus so much of their message on "prosperity" and "monetary blessing" that those who listen get the impression that the only sign of God's blessing is measured in cash, cars, and toys. This is neither biblical nor healthy. At the other end of the continuum, there are those who never want to talk about material blessings. They fear the accusation, "All you care about is money." The reality is that God has many ways he chooses to bless his children and one of them is with material resources. There is not a cause-and-effect guarantee that if we walk in obedience we will get more earthly stuff. But, there are many times God does choose to give resources to his followers. When he does this, he expects them to be wise and generous managers of these material goods.

Read Psalm 112:3, 5, 9

7. What are some of the material blessings God has provided for you and those you love?

What are some ways you can show God that you are thankful for these gifts?

8. The psalmist declares that one of the things obedient followers of God do is "scatter abroad their gifts to the poor." What are some of the ways we can identify and meet the needs of those who are less fortunate?

Character Blessings

When God finds people who are totally devoted to him, he blesses their character. He builds these people up. In a very real sense, God makes these people bright lights in a world filled with darkness. In the confusion and chaos of this world God still wants his light to shine, and the way he often chooses to illuminate things is through our character.

Think about how these character qualities can pierce the darkness of our relational world. Read each one slowly and imagine the blessings that will come to this world as Christ followers overflow with each of these:

- Graciousness
- Compassion
- Righteousness
- Generosity
- Justice
- Courage

These are just a sample of the character blessings God wants to infuse into your life. These are rare in our world, but so desperately needed.

Read Psalm 112:4 – 9 and Galatians 5:22 – 23

9. What is one of the character qualities listed in these passages that you see alive in your heart, and what is an example of how this quality is growing in you?

10. What is one character quality found in these passages (or elsewhere in the Bible) that you really want to see grow in your life? What is one practical step you can take to be part of God's work of developing this quality within you?

Celebrating and Being Celebrated

Some of your group members were courageous and expressed a specific character quality they see God growing in their lives (see question 9). Take time as a group to give examples (or share stories) of how you see that same character quality alive and developing in their lives.

Loving and Being Loved

In this session we focused on how God brings family blessings which pour from one generation to the next. If you have a parent, grandparent, or significant person (they don't have to be family) who has been a conduit of God's blessing into your life, let them know, very specifically, how God has imparted bless-ing in your life through them. This will be a small way to let the current of blessing flow the other way. Pray that God will uplift and encourage them through your words.

Serving and Being Served

Take a moment to do a material blessing inventory. Make a list of at least five things you have (think specifically of the kinds of things you can share with others).

My Material Blessing Inventory

Item _____

Item _____

Item _____

Item _____

Item _____

After you have made your list, write down three of four prac-tical ways you could "scatter your gifts" to help others. Be cre-ative in this process. An old car might be donated and fixed up as a gift for a needy person. A spare room might become the place an adopted child would be raised. An item around the house that is never used could be sold and the proceeds given to a local shelter. A monthly raise could become food, clothing, and education for a child in another country though a sponsor pro-gram. A family cottage might be made available to a struggling young couple or a single mother for a vacation they could never afford and would never forget. A boat could be made available to take a group of inner-city kids out to a lake. Be thoughtful and prayerful as you look at what you have and consider how you might scatter some blessing.

Some ways I could leverage my resources to bless others:

Idea _____

Idea _____

Idea _____

Idea _____

Dwelling Together in Unity

PSALM 133

Have you ever sat around a kitchen table with family members and felt the sweetness of the loving community that exists when there is unity? Maybe you have been in a meeting with church members and felt a common vision and a sense of corporate calling; it was like your hearts were beating together and you knew that God was pleased and great things were going to happen because you were together. Perhaps you have experienced moments around a roaring fire with close friends sharing life and laughter, and you just knew that God was rejoicing because his children were drinking in the pleasant reality that unity is not only possible, it is his plan. There are few joys in this life richer and more memorable than the times we dwell together in unity.

Most of us have also experienced moments that were the polar opposite. A family sits around the dinner table blanketed by cold silence or heaped with cutting words. Church members meet to make plans for ministry, but things erupt into a series of arguments and slanderous accusations based on hidden agendas and selfish desires. Friends gather for fellowship and before you know it old wounds are opened and the gloves come off. In all of life, there are few pains greater than disunity.

Jesus was so serious about the importance of unity among his people that he prayed:

> I pray ... that all of them may be one, Father, just as you are in me and I am in you. May they also be in us so that the world may believe that you have sent me. I have given them the glory that you gave me, that they may be one as we are one: I in them and you in me. May they be brought to complete unity to let the world know that you sent me and have loved them even as you have loved me. (John 17:20–23)

Earlier in the gospel of John, Jesus says, "A new command I give you: Love one another. As I have loved you, so you must love one another. By this all men will know that you are my disciples, if you love one another" (John 13:34–35). Jesus is clear that the way his followers love each other will mirror to the world that we are his followers. In a world that accepts and sometimes encourages disunity, followers of Christ are called to dwell together in unity.

Making the Connection

1. Tell about a time that you experienced the sweetness of unity with a group of people. What made this time so memorable and pleasant?

Knowing and Being Known

Read Psalm 133
2. God's vision and goal for his people is that we would dwell together in the goodness of unity. What are signs and indications that a group of Christ followers are experiencing true unity?

What are some signs that disunity is present among God's people?

I Celebrate Your Gifting and Calling

In Psalm 133 David is declaring there is something wonderful, special, even supernatural about relationships in the body of Christ. He uses a rich word picture to describe one of the ways God's people can experience and strengthen our unity. David compares the blessedness of unity to an epic moment in the life of Aaron, the high priest of Israel. It might not connect for us, but it made a lot of sense to the people of David's day (Exodus 29:7).

When Aaron received his call and formal ordination, he was anointed with oil mixed with spices. This anointing was a picture that God was setting this man aside for a specific ministry and calling: he would offer sacrifices to cover the sins of the people, he would be a servant of God. As the oil poured over his head, down his beard, and onto the collar of his robe, it symbolized the presence of the Holy Spirit and authenticated Aaron's calling to the priesthood.

Every follower of Christ is gifted and called to ministry. One of the things that unites us is that we are one body, in Christ. Each part of the body has a job, responsibility, ministry. We experience the sweetness of unity as we celebrate the calling and gifts God has placed in our brothers and sisters. Each person in God's family is valuable, needed, and essential to the health of the body. When we affirm the gifts, the calling, and the ministry of the Christ followers around us, it is like the precious anointing oil of the Spirit is flowing again. The sweet and undeniable scent of unity is in the air.

Read Psalm 133:1 – 2 and I Corinthians 12:12 – 26

3. In 1 Corinthians 12 the apostle Paul paints a picture of unity in the church (the body of Christ). According to this passage, what are signs that unity exists among the members of the body?

What are signs that we are not experiencing the unity God desires?

4. Just as Aaron had a specific priestly ministry, every follower of Jesus is given a spiritual gift (Romans 12:6–8; 1 Corinthians 12:7–11; Ephesians 4:11). What is one spiritual gift God has given you, and how have you used this gift to serve God and people?

5. We often live with a sense of excitement about serving God in some fresh new way. What is an area of service you believe God may call you to sometime in the future?

How can your group members pray for you and encourage you as you investigate and open yourself to this new area of service?

I Celebrate God's Overflow from Your Life

The second image of Christian unity that David uses also bears some explanation. Mount Hermon is the highest point in all Israel, standing 9,230 feet above sea level. Because of its height, it is snowcapped for much of the year; it also collects an enormous amount of dew throughout the night and early morning. However, by mid-morning and noonday—when the sun strikes the mountain snow and dew—life-giving, precious water runs down the mountain, providing the arid, dusty regions below with desperately needed irrigation.

Again David is painting a rich word picture. When we are among God's people and experience the goodness of unity, it is like the life-giving waters that flow down from Mount Hermon. The presence of other Christ followers becomes a continual infusion of relational water to refresh our parched souls. What a gift it is when we live with a level of unity that brings this kind of relational refreshment! When this happens, we can look at our sisters and brothers in Christ and say, "God is using you to overflow his goodness into my life!"

Read Psalm 133:1 – 3

6. We all know Christ followers who just overflow with the presence and goodness of God. They are like a little traveling Mount Hermon that brings refreshment wherever it goes. These are people we love to be around. Who is one person you would describe this way, and what happens in your heart when you are around them?

7. What can we do to live in deeper unity with others in God's family so that we will become a source of life-giving refreshment to the people around us?

Read Acts 2:42 – 47

Community for All Generations

God's concern for unity among his people runs like a thread through the entire Bible. At the birth of the New Testament church in Acts 2, the picture becomes clearer. Right after Pentecost and the coming of the Holy Spirit, the church begins to grow ... rapidly! Then we get this little peek, just six short verses, of what God is doing. It's an amazing picture of unity and community. This is oil on the beard of Aaron, dew on Mount Hermon stuff!

Four elements of a unified and healthy church immediately rose to the surface:

- **They devoted themselves to the teaching of God's Word.** The teaching came out of the Scriptures and it was strong, accurate, and powerful. They gathered as a body so they could learn from God together. They not only attended and listened, but they applied the teaching to their lives.
- **They committed to regular fellowship.** Fellowship does wonderful things. It minimizes your loneliness, multiples your joys, divides your sorrows, expands your wisdom, and encourages your spirit. The early church discovered that being together was essential to their health and unity.
- **They shared communion together.** The first Lord's Supper was around a table; it was intimate ... a picture of community. The early believers experienced the powerful reminder of the life and work of Jesus every time they gathered to break the bread and drink from the cup.
- **They prayed in community.** When the early followers of Jesus came together, they would regularly call out to God in corporate prayer. These prayers unleashed the power of God.

8. How does devoting ourselves to the teaching of God's Word lead to strong community and unity among God's people?

59

9. Small groups are places of both learning and fellowship. How has the fellowship of this particular group strengthened you in your faith?

10. Followers of Christ all over the world break the bread, drink from the cup, and remember Jesus as they celebrate communion. What is it about the Lord's Supper that has such a unifying and community-building power in the church?

11. How have you seen prayer build unity, tear down walls, or develop community among followers of Christ?

Celebrating and Being Celebrated

As the anointing oil poured over Aaron, those nearby surely celebrated his gifts and calling in ministry. As we share life with other Christ followers, it is appropriate to affirm and rejoice when they faithfully use their gifts and abilities in service to God and people. Take time in your group to bless, affirm, and celebrate the ways some of your group members are using their gifts for God's glory.

Loving and Being Loved

In 1 Corinthians 12 we read about those members of the body who are not readily noticed—the modest type. Yet we are called to honor all the members of the body. As a group identify a couple of ministries in your church or community that are more behind the scenes and often go unnoticed. Perhaps it's a technical ministry, the church nursery, an outreach to shut-ins and the hospitalized, or some other ministry that gets very little spotlight time. Plan some way you can honor and extend love to these faithful servants who often go overlooked.

Serving and Being Served

Consider closing this final session with a time of mutual service by celebrating communion together (if your church tradition allows this). Have someone prepare the elements and as you serve each other the bread, offer words of institution such as, "The body of Christ broken for you." As you serve each other the cup, say, "The blood of Christ shed for you." Let this be a time of experiencing the unity we have together around the table of Jesus.

Session One – The Road to Blessedness
PSALM I

Questions 2–3

If you ask a good parent what he or she really wants for a child, they will tell you they want their little one to grow up full of joy, contentment, purpose, and fulfillment in all of life. To use the biblical term, they want their child to experience blessedness. What more would a parent want? This is the same thing that God wants for you. He wants you to experience blessedness and prosperity in your spirit. Abundant life, Jesus called it in John 10:10 (NASB). So, he says, in effect, "I am going to mark a road for you to follow and it is called obedience. If you follow the road to obedience, you will ultimately be overwhelmed by how much blessedness I will pour into your life. If you make the right choices and stay on the right road, blessedness is guaranteed to you. Not painless living, not problem-free living, but blessedness."

Blessedness doesn't require blissful circumstances. It transcends circumstances. It comes from a right relationship with God, which in turn impacts every other relationship. Blessedness is what the human heart truly longs to experience. At some point along the way each person must become convinced, to the core of their being, that obedience is the only road that leads ultimately to blessedness.

When we come to this point of realization, it is going to change our whole perspective on our relationship to God. We begin to think, "How can it be? God is so full of love and concern for me that he wants me to experience blessedness. I matter so much to God that he clearly outlines a road map, a blueprint for me to follow. He gives me the Holy Spirit and brothers and sisters and a lot of other assets to encourage me to take that road because he wants to ensure that blessedness will prevail in my life."

This reality should motivate us toward obedience. When we face those practical, everyday choices and crossroads, we should long to be obedient because we know blessedness is at the end of the road.

Questions 4–6

If we are honest about it, some of the counsel the world gives sounds pretty good. We can be tempted by the offers made by those who stand at the crossroads and make all kinds of promises. But the psalmist says that only the road named obedience will lead to true blessedness. We have a choice to make. The wise person will not be tricked by the slogans and the counsel of ungodly people.

Much of our future is determined by who we listen to and who we don't. Christian character demands, at a certain point in time, that we make a calculated decision not to listen to certain people, certain voices, certain individuals espousing certain values. Wisdom is not just listening to the right people, but ignoring the wrong people.

When we stay on God's path, through faith in Jesus Christ, we are assured the ultimate blessedness: eternal life in heaven with God. The ultimate barrenness is an eternity in hell. Real people will either be in heaven or hell. Real people take the path of obedience or disobedience, which leads to blessedness or barrenness. This makes the need for wisdom in who we listen to and what path we take of ultimate importance.

When we hear the voice of God and follow it, we end up on the road of blessedness. When we listen to the voices of the wicked and mocking, we end up on the path of barrenness.

For example: When people take the road to obedience with their money and live with generous hearts and hands, they experience the blessedness that can come from God with respect to their resources. When they take the road of arrogance, selfishness, and disobedience with their money, they can face calamity and heartache. It is the same thing with our bodies. The road marked obedience says if we follow God's Word in how we treat ourselves, it will lead to blessedness physically. Of course we understand that we are not immune to physical afflictions and we are all going to die someday.

But the general promise in Scripture is blessedness as a reward for treating our bodies in a way that honors God. The opposite is also true. If we treat our bodies poorly and forget that they are the temple of the Holy Spirit, we can suffer the consequences. The same is true with our spiritual gifts. If we use spiritual gifts the way the road marked obedience tells us to use them, we will experience the blessedness of being useful and fruitful for God. If we don't, and we hide our gifts and talents from God and others, we miss out on God's blessings. If we take the pathway marked obedience we increase our future blessedness factor ... every single time.

Questions 7–9

As the voices of the world cry out to us to walk on the road of disobedience, where do we go for good counsel? For one thing, there are wise and godly people who can give great insight for living. We need to stay near these people and learn all we can.

In addition to these people, we need to go to God's Word. This source of heavenly wisdom will guide and direct us to the way of blessedness every time. There is no area of life that the Bible does not address and offer direction. What a gift to have the very words of God recorded so that we can avoid the consequences and heartache of ending up on the road of barrenness.

Question 10–11

This picture of blessedness is a tree that is productive; it provides life-giving fruit; it is prosperous. It reminds me of what Jesus said in John 4:14: when we are rightly related to him and we experience this thing called blessedness, it is like a well springing up in our soul. It never, never, never runs dry. God's mercies are new every morning—fresh, dynamic, ongoing, a continual surprise.

Blessedness carries with it the idea of youthfulness and productiveness. Being useful and productive for God intensifies those feelings of blessedness. A whole dimension of blessedness is missing from our lives if we have not yet discovered the joy of being productive and useful for God—in other people's lives, and for his kingdom.

The psalmist also says a blessed person will be like a tree whose leaves do not wither. Blessed people don't wilt easily; they just keep rebounding. When everyone else counts them down and out, they say, "I'm not done. I'm not out." They possess an eternal source of courage, a deep sense of optimism because they are rightly related to an omnipotent God.

A blessed man or a blessed woman bears fruit. The fruit of character keeps growing in their lives. They have that blessed feeling of saying, "Two years ago I would have fallen for that; I would have run full speed down that sinful road. But I wouldn't do that now. I have changed. My character, my disposition, my choices are all changing."

The whole world is yearning for this thing called blessedness. The psalmist predicts that certain people are going to experience vast amounts of blessedness in the future. It will come as they walk the road of obedience in the things of God. As they do, the life-giving water of the Holy Spirit will fill them to overflowing. Not only will they be refreshed, but they will overflow into the lives of others ... now that is blessedness!

Session Two – Godly Guilt
PSALM 38

Questions 1–3

The tendency toward being either very sensitive or tough-skinned can begin early in life. This natural disposition can carry into how we respond to feelings of guilt. I noticed this early on in the lives of my two kids. Back in 1986, seven astronauts tragically lost their lives when the space shuttle *Challenger* exploded after takeoff. About a week later I was sitting in my study with the kids looking at the latest newsmagazines. The cover of one magazine showed the shuttle exploding and the cover of the other showed pictures of the seven who died. One of my kids started to shed some tears and said, "It is just really, really sad, isn't it, Dad?" I said, "You know, it is really, really sad." My other child said, "You know, they had the choice; they didn't have to go up there if they didn't want to. They knew it was dangerous."

Here are two children, born to the same parents, raised in the same home, but very different. Some people are more sensitive and others are more thick-skinned. Both are fine. But we need to be careful that this natural disposition does not spin out of control, one way or the other, when it comes to dealing with guilt.

Many scholars believe that David wrote Psalm 38 with his sin with Bathsheba and her husband, Uriah, in mind. It was an awful chapter of David's life that included the sins of adultery and murder, among others. Another interesting contextual note is that some commentators believe that this psalm was written about the time Absalom, David's son, was trying to take over the throne from David. This could explain David's references to enemies and traps that are being set for him.

Questions 4–6

David's lament and honest cries in verses 3–7 seem to be expressing pain and suffering on both a physical and emotional level. Sometimes it is hard to tell if he is talking about the condition of his body, his heart, or both. But through the whole passage it is clear that David is facing deep internal trauma. Finally, in verse 8 he culminates this list of suffering by declaring that he is utterly crushed!

Some people tend to live in verse 8 all of the time. Anything can happen and they feel crushed by guilt. If they get a traffic ticket, are late for work, or burn the toast … the world comes crashing down on them. They are dealing with a misdemeanor, but they feel like it is a capital offense. This is when Satan, whom the Bible calls the accuser, loves to slip in. He loves to exaggerate things and bring all kinds of emotional and psychological havoc into our lives. When this happens, it is probably not appropriate and godly guilt. God does not want us anxious and obsessive over trivial things in life. Those who are particularly tender in heart and very sensitive need to be sure the enemy does not capitalize on these moments and cause them to fixate on false guilt.

On the other hand, there are those who can't even relate to verse 8. They have never felt crushed by the weight of sin. Some have never groaned over their own rebellious hearts. Some have committed major felonies in the face of a holy God, and it does not even faze them. They can rattle off a list of five reasons why they did what they did and why they don't have to feel guilty or lose sleep over it. These people believe a different lie of the enemy. When they sin, Satan comes along and tells them, "It's no big deal; don't worry about it." In their case, a good dose of godly guilt will wake them up to the need for confession and repentance.

All through the history of the Bible very holy and righteous people were aware of their need for grace and forgiveness. Job, who was called the most righteous man in his generation, cried out to the Lord, "I repent in dust and ashes" (Job 42:6). Isaiah saw God and said, "Woe to me! I am ruined! For I am a man of unclean lips" (Isaiah 6:5). John the Baptist said, "After me will come one more powerful than I, the thongs of whose sandals I am not worthy to stoop down and untie" (Mark 1:7). Peter declared, "Go away from me, Lord; I am a sinful man" (Luke 5:8). Countless men and women who have walked before us have fallen on their faces, expressed their brokenness before God, and pleaded for his forgiveness and mercy.

Questions 7–8

David is crying out to God with a broken heart, in essence saying: "My feelings are an open book before you. You know what I am going through. I don't feel your friendship. I feel your judgment. My heart throbs, my strength fails me, I am nearly wiped out, blinded over this thing." David feels isolated from God. This is relational trauma at its height. He is also feeling disconnected from friends and family. His loved ones stand at a distance. He feels vulnerable to his enemies. It seems that every one of David's relationships has been turned upside down. Sin can do that. It impacts and infects every aspect of our lives.

One interesting note is that David feels ostracized and excluded from the fellowship of others who follow God. This happens sometimes to people who are living in deep places of sin. They will begin to say things like, "Everyone at the church is judging me; they are a bunch of hypocrites!" Or, "I just can't be around Christians right now because they are treating me poorly."

It can be true that some followers of Christ do reject and exclude people when they are struggling with sin. But, more often, the issue is that the person indulging in sin will twist reality and claim that other believers are driving them out and judging them wrongly. They find it easier to call other believers judgmental than to come back to the fellowship, admit their sin, and stay in community seeking to rebuild credibility. We need to commit to stay in community with other Christ followers, even when — especially when — we are battling with sin.

Questions 9–11

When followers of Christ fall into sin, godly guilt always comes. It is a gift, a heavenly warning mechanism to protect us from further damage. If we resist these promptings and warnings, we can end up crushed, feeling separated and isolated from God, sometimes suffering even physical or emotional nausea. But when we confess our sins and turn from them, the guilt is lifted and we feel free, restored, forgiven.

When we understand the miraculous deliverance of God and the freedom from sin he accomplished for us on the cross, our desire to sin decreases. When we acknowledge the offense that sin is to the God we love, our interest in forbidden fruit lessens. As we drink in the amazing grace of Jesus, we are not quick to run right back out and dive off the same diving board into the same pit of sin again and again.

This is not to say we will never repeat sins; we will battle temptation as long as we have breath in our bodies. But the trauma that comes with repeating the same sinful behavior over and over becomes wearisome. The weight of godly guilt when we keep living as a repeat offender can get heavy. With time, we realize that walking in obedience is actually the path to freedom and joy.

David learned this lesson and sought to confess and get back on the right track. He as much as admitted to God, "I knew your will and chose to do mine. I knew your way and went mine." We can learn from his example. We need to admit our sinfulness to God, and even to each other. In Jeremiah 31:34 we read these life-changing words from the mouth and heart of God: "For I will forgive their wickedness and will remember their sins no more."

Every Christ follower ought to memorize this verse to throw back at Satan when he says, "You are still guilty. God can't forgive you!" When we confess our sins and accept the grace of Jesus, God has a case of divine amnesia. And he can use our guilt to bring us to this place of confession and transformation.

Session Three – Choosing to Trust God
PSALM 56

Question 1

Can you see the wisdom of God in allowing us to have a psalm like Psalm 56 in our Bible? You see, the great King David occasionally took the same roller-coaster ride that we take. He was a man of great faith—and also great fear. He loved God, but he had his ups and downs.

Every believer who has ever lived has done daily battle with fear and faith. We have all found ourselves trembling when we should have been trusting, or trusting one moment and trembling the next. We are not mutants or misfits. We are simply men and women, made of flesh and blood, all susceptible to these same struggles and human frailties. Psalm 56 hits us right where we live. It echoes the same kind of conversations so many of us have with God throughout an ordinary day.

Questions 4–6

The psalm begins with a plea for mercy. The mighty man of valor, giant-killing David, cries out to God with brutal honesty, "Give me a break; enough is enough; lighten up. I don't think I can handle what you are asking me to handle much longer. Be gracious to me because I feel like I am at the breaking point." You can almost feel David's pain and struggle as he bemoans his afflictions at the hands of his enemies. Though he might have never said these kinds of things in public, he feels free to say them in private.

Then, all of a sudden, he catches himself, as if he realizes, "What am I doing? I am caving in again. I am giving way to feelings of fear. I am expecting the worst. I am making up awful endings to the trials that are facing me. I am becoming convinced that God is going to fail me." So, in verses 3–4 David deliberately changes his focus and turns his attention to the trustworthiness of God. It is as though he says, "Wait a minute. I wasn't born yesterday. God has never failed me. Why am I going down this track that leads to nowhere?" As he remembers God's faithfulness, his heart begins to calm, his spirit lifts, his faith deepens.

But just when it seems his confidence is finally restored, his focus shifts again—from the sufficiency of God to the severity of his problem. In verses 5–6, he fixates once more on the oppression of his enemies: "All day long they twist my words; they are always plotting to harm me. They conspire, they lurk, they watch my steps, eager to take my life." A few moments ago David was calling his enemies "mere men." Now they are man-eating monsters.

Is David schizophrenic? Is he losing his mind? Is he a man of weak faith? No! He is just like you and me, a person with real faith and real fear bouncing around in the same heart.

Questions 7–8

Choosing to walk and live by faith requires a type of mental tenacity that most people don't associate with Christianity—a kind of spiritual courage and determination usually reserved for athletic competitions or battlefields. It means focusing our minds, over and over again, on the fact of the trustworthiness of God.

Fear keeps flooding into our minds without an invitation. Satan sees to that. But faith in God's character and trustworthiness, the ability to trust him when things around us look bad, that kind of trust demands all the discipline we can muster. It takes years of practice. It takes believing in God even when everyone around us calls us foolish and fanatical. It is a tough duty, only doable with God's strength.

We are all given ample opportunities to battle through the faith-and-fear roller-coaster experiences of life. When they come, we can learn, more and more over time, to trust in God ... no matter what. Consider some of these opportunities:

- **A loved one becomes very ill.** You find yourself bouncing between deep trust in God's presence and power in the situation and fear over the potential loss of this precious person.
- **Finances are getting tight.** One moment you declare your trust in God's provision and care for you. Soon thereafter you honestly wonder if you will have what you need to pay the bills and provide for your family.
- **A relationship is on the rocks.** You are confident God can heal and restore this relationship. In the very same breath you worry that things will never get back to the way they use to be.

In all these situations, and countless more, we have a choice. We can be ruled and controlled by fear and worry, or we can make a decision to walk in faith and confidence in God.

Questions 9–11

David lists some significant facts that pertain to the trustworthiness of God, basic truths that should inspire and encourage us all. Consider these:

- **God is for me.** Almighty God is on my side. He is cheering me on, is inclined to act favorably toward me. He really cares.
- **God relieves my fear.** David is clear that he does not believe God always takes away our problems, but God can remove our fear, even in the face of enemies. We can live sanely, confidently, and even joyfully despite our problems.
- **God watches over me.** Even when we feel alone, we can know that God has his eye on us. What can people do to me when God is watching over me? Why should I feel vulnerable and exposed? I am the object of his loving and watchful eye.

Session Four – Fear Not
PSALM 91

Questions 1–3

Some of the people in your group are only dealing with annoying minor-league fears. Others are facing huge fears and struggles in their lives. One key to this study is making sure that people are not comparing the magnitude of their fear-producing situations. That's not the point of Psalm 91. It is about helping all of us walk and live through our fears, be they small or large.

A friend once said to me, "It is not the sharks that get me; it's the guppies!" This person had a lot of little fears, but they added up. Whether a person faces pestering fears that irritate, pressing fears that hang like dark clouds overhead, or the panic-producing fears that paralyze, all of us need relief. The message of this psalm offers answers for whatever fears a person faces.

Questions 4–5

God wants his children to be optimistic, self-confident, courageous, trusting. He grieves when his sons and daughters are crippled with fear, incapacitated by anxiety, immobilized by worry. One of God's passions is to free us from these debilitating bonds. Psalm 91 is one of the best passages in the entire Bible to help us overcome fear.

The psalm begins, in the first two verses, with a focus on God. This is the starting place for overcoming all kinds of fear ... it must be. When we recognize that God is our refuge, our shelter, our fortress, we grow more confident. The military language in this passage is not accidental. Fear attacks us like an enemy, but God will be a fortress. What comfort!

Questions 6–7

In verse 3 and then again in verses 5–7 the psalmist seems to make the point that he understands why some of us wrestle with varying levels of fear. In essence he says, "I know what the real world is like. I live in it too." He understands that the world can be evil, cruel, and cold. He has seen and experienced the random strikes of adversity and tragedy that crash into people's lives. He knows what it feels like to wonder when the other shoe is going to drop. He is not writing from an ivory tower of protection. But he is also supremely confident that the God who has promised to be our refuge, Savior, and protector can take care of his children.

Verse 3 talks about the fowler's snare. In those days, bird hunters would sprinkle some seeds under a tree, then hang a weighted net from the limbs. When a flock of birds came to feed, the hunters would cut the rope, trapping the birds beneath the fallen net. The unsuspecting birds were so grateful for the free lunch they little suspected they would soon be someone else's lunch! The psalmist is saying, "Sometimes you feel like that trapped bird. You didn't even see it coming!" But God can set you free. He has the power and prerogative to do so.

The psalmist goes on to give a list of the fear-producing things we can face in life and how God is able to deliver us. Terror can strike, but God can protect. Violence might be close at hand, but God can cover us. People around us can face tragedy, but God can spare us. This psalm is not a flat-out guarantee that every problem we face will be swept away. But it is a profound reminder that God is present, he is powerful, and he promises to have his hand on the lives of his children. Sometimes he will deliver us. At other times, he will stand at our side and help us through. But, we can be sure he will never leave us alone. He will cover us with his wings ... what an intimate picture of God's protecting presence!

Question 8

Those who are absolutely paralyzed by fear might want to pray for eyes to see the spiritual world around them. Not only is God watching over them and covering them with his wings, but he sends angels to protect them. Hebrews 1:14 tells us that God has commissioned ministering spirits to come at our point of need and render service to his children. If we could only see, just one time, the angelic hosts God has sent to guard us we would be freed from wandering in the wastelands of fear.

Angels surround us, guiding and protecting us, fending off Satan's random attacks. We all have stories about life's "close calls." We may not ever know, this side of eternity, how many times we have been spared because of heavenly intervention on our behalf.

Questions 9–10

I have a discipline that God has called me to practice. I write out, formally, longhand, a full notebook page of prayers each day. This works for me. I am not suggesting that everyone should do this, but it could prove helpful for some. One of the reasons I do this is that I can see my words in print, right on the page:

"Lord, I am finding myself caving in to fear again this morning. Fear about my children's safety and future. Fear about what I will preach. Fear about future ministry plans. In your very presence, I am deliberately choosing to refuse to wander today in the wastelands of fear."

Then I might underline parts of the prayer that stir my heart with conviction and truth and continue to write:

"God, I am deliberately choosing, at this point in time, in your presence, that I will not live in the wastelands of fear today. I am not

going to imagine all kinds of worst-case scenarios. I am not going to spend time making up nightmares and replaying them in my mind. I am not going to live that way today. I am, therefore, making the deliberate choice to walk in faith today."

If I were studying and meditating on Psalm 91, I might write:

"Because of who you are, and because of what your angels are doing, and because of the power of prayer, I will not live in fear! You are the Most High, Almighty God, and I will seek to walk in your shadow. You have given your angels charge over me, and they are encamped around me. Give me a vision and awareness of your protection around me. I cast my cares, worries, and fears on you. I am not going to just tell you my problem; I am going to give you my problem right now. I am going to place it at your feet and leave it there. Today I am going to follow you and not let fear win the day. In the name of Jesus, Amen!"

Session Five – The Blessings of Obedience
PSALM 112

Questions 2–3

What does a mature Christian look like? What does "spiritual maturity" mean? One helpful definition: someone who takes God and his Word seriously. Psalm 112 begins by making it clear that blessings begin with the fear of the Lord and taking his commandments (his Word) seriously. This psalm and session are about blessing, but the blessings we will talk about come as we walk in obedience.

Psalm 112 focuses its spotlight on deeply committed followers of Jesus. These are people who seek to follow God completely, as best they know how; women and men who have long since decided that there is no one, or nothing else in this world, worthy of committing their entire life to other than God and his purposes. These are people who are offering up their lives as a living sacrifice; who revere God, who exalt God, who relate to God earnestly, submissively, lovingly, respectfully, and wholeheartedly.

People like this have discovered that doing God's bidding faithfully, over a long period of time, brings the greatest amount of fulfillment we could possibly know in this life. They have already found out that faithfulness to Jesus Christ is the only way to fly and that following the leading of the Holy Spirit fills life with adventure and surprises. These are the true thrill seekers. They know that there is no extreme sport or heart-thumping rush in this world that comes close to touching the exhilaration of walking obediently with God and receiving the blessings that follow.

Questions 4–6

The Bible regularly notes God's promise to spill his kindness into the lives of those who are wholly devoted to him, but it does not stop there. Because of our devotion to God, he not only lavishly pours out his blessings on our lives, but causes our cups to overflow to children and generations not yet born.

There is a principle called "associated blessings" and "associated curses." This is the idea that when a man or woman is wholly devoted to God, the blessings of God are so present in their lives that other people receive the overflow. If you know the Old Testament story of Joseph, you get the idea. Everywhere Joseph went, he prospered ... and those around him were caught up in the overflow. When people walk in passionate obedience to God, the blessings of heaven pour down on spouses, family members, business associates, friends, and neighbors; all sorts of people benefit.

In a similar way, people who defy God, who regularly disobey him, who ignore his principles, and who do violence to his kingdom, face his discipline. When this happens, those who are in the immediate vicinity can be impacted by the consequences. For example, just as blessings and godly habits can be passed down through the generations, so bad habits and rebellious lifestyles can also be passed down from parent to child and beyond. This is a sad reality, but it is something we have all seen on far too many occasions.

Questions 7–8

A major theme in Scripture is that God has a way of rewarding people materially and financially as they are faithful children and obedient stewards. Sadly, God's gracious generosity has been perverted by some. This confusion of a biblical principle with an earthly strategy—what has come to be called prosperity theology—goes something like this: *God has promised to provide a material blessing to those who walk and live in faith. If you have faith, God must give you more stuff.* People who buy into prosperity theology devote themselves to God so that he will be obligated to bless them materially. It is a cause-and-effect, faith-for-dollars deal. And if blessings cease, these people feel justified in throwing their faith out the window ... since it is no longer paying out.

The Bible does not guarantee that those who follow God faithfully will be rich. It does not even say that they will never struggle with financial needs. What it says is that *one of the ways* God blesses those who walk obediently is through material resources. True Christ followers worship God for who he is. They love God because of what Jesus did on the cross. Even if they had to live with a modest amount of earthly goods, they would follow, love, and give praise to God anyway.

Session Six — Dwelling Together in Unity
PSALM 133

Questions 1–2

Psalm 133 is a short psalm, only three verses. David begins by saying it is good and pleasant when brothers "dwell together in unity" (NASB). Note he didn't say, "How good and how pleasant it is for brothers to dwell together." Sometimes dwelling together can be anything but unifying—just ask kids who have shared a room, soldiers who have shared barracks, or college students who have been crammed into a dorm together with people they don't click with. The point is, "goodness" and "pleasantness" come when there is unity.

When Christ followers dwell together in unity, it is as though they experience and enjoy an outpouring of God's anointing. It can't be manufactured by human effort, something we can create or manipulate. It is otherworldly in a way, alien to the experience of people outside the family of God who might understand friendship, but not this kind of unified community.

Questions 3–5

Not everyone is aware of their unique and God-given spiritual gift. It might be helpful to read the following three passages and highlight the specific gifts of the Spirit (italicized here for easy reference). There may be some who are using a gift but don't even realize the specific name of the gift. Don't split hairs over this. The goal is to let people articulate a gift or way they are serving God and others.

> We have different gifts, according to the grace given us. If a man's gift is *prophesying*, let him use it in proportion to his faith. If it is *serving*, let him serve; if it is *teaching*, let him teach; if it is *encouraging*, let him encourage; if it is *contributing* to the needs of others, let him give generously; if it is *leadership*, let him govern diligently; if it is *showing mercy*, let him do it cheerfully. (Romans 12:6–8, italics added)

> Now to each one the manifestation of the Spirit is given for the common good. To one there is given through the Spirit the message of *wisdom*, to another the message of *knowledge* by means of the same Spirit, to another *faith* by the same Spirit, to another gifts of *healing* by that one Spirit, to another *miraculous powers*, to another *prophecy*, to another *distinguishing between spirits*, to another *speaking in different kinds of tongues*, and to still another the *interpretation of tongues*. All these are the work of one and the same Spirit, and he gives them to each one, just as he determines. (1 Corinthians 12:7–11, italics added)

> It was he who gave some to be *apostles*, some to be *prophets*, some to be *evangelists*, and some to be *pastors* and *teachers*. (Ephesians 4:11, italics added)

Questions 8–11

God wants to do great things in all of us, to start a revolution that will continue our entire lives. If we want to be greatly used, we must be thoroughly trained and nourished spiritually, and that comes through the teaching of God's Word. This happens as we gather for weekend and midweek services of worship, as we read good books, study the Bible, listen to tapes and radio programs, and hunger to learn more.

Fellowship is also important. Being part of a formal small group or informal fellowship allows us to walk together, care for each other, and sharpen each other. This should always be a high priority. If a person has been a follower of Christ for fifty years or five days, fellowship is a gift to each of us.

Jesus instituted communion among his followers. While he was with a small group of brothers with whom he had walked for three years, he said, "Do this in remembrance of me." They had traveled together, shared meals, faced opposition, wept, laughed, and shared life. When Jesus broke the bread and passed the cup, as they sang hymns together at that last supper, it is easy to imagine Jesus saying, "How good and how pleasant it is when brothers dwell together in unity."

Prayer flowed naturally among the early believers. It should be so for us as well. Authentic conversations with God should erupt as we are together. A need arises; we pray. A joy is shared, so we stop and celebrate, giving thanks to God with a brother or sister. Sin is confessed; we pray for forgiveness, strength, and the power of the Spirit to help this person walk in obedience. Prayer should mark any gathering of God's people.

We value your thoughts about what you've just read. Please share them with us. You'll find contact information in the back of this book.

WILLOW
Willow Creek Association

Willow Creek Association
Vision, Training, Resources for Prevailing Churches

This resource was created to serve you and to help you build a local church that prevails. It is just one of many ministry tools that are part of the Willow Creek Resources® line, published by the Willow Creek Association together with Zondervan.

The Willow Creek Association (WCA) was created in 1992 to serve a rapidly growing number of churches from across the denominational spectrum that are committed to helping unchurched people become fully devoted followers of Christ. Membership in the WCA now numbers over 12,000 Member Churches worldwide from more than ninety denominations.

The Willow Creek Association links like-minded Christian leaders with each other and with strategic vision, training, and resources in order to help them build prevailing churches designed to reach their redemptive potential. Here are some of the ways the WCA does that.

- **The Leadership Summit**—a once a year, two-and-a-half-day conference to envision and equip Christians with leadership gifts and responsibilities. Presented live at Willow Creek as well as via satellite broadcast to over 130 locations across North America, this event is designed to increase the leadership effectiveness of pastors, ministry staff, volunteer church leaders, and Christians in the marketplace.

- **Ministry-Specific Conferences**—throughout each year the WCA hosts a variety of conferences and training events—both at Willow Creek's main campus and offsite, across the U.S., and around the world—targeting church leaders and volunteers in ministry-specific areas such as: small groups, preaching and teaching, the arts, children, students, volunteers, stewardship, etc.

- **Willow Creek Resources®**—provides churches with trusted and field-tested ministry resources in such areas as leadership, evangelism, spiritual formation, spiritual gifts, small groups, stewardship, student ministry, children's ministry, the use of the arts—drama, media, contemporary music—and more.

- **WCA Member Benefits**—includes substantial discounts to WCA training events, a 20 percent discount on all Willow Creek Resources®, *Defining Moments* monthly audio journal for leaders, quarterly *Willow* magazine, access to a Members-Only section on WillowNet, monthly communications, and more. Member Churches also receive special discounts and premier services through WCA's growing number of ministry partners—Select Service Providers—and save an average of $500 annually depending on the level of engagement.

For specific information about WCA conferences, resources, membership, and other ministry services contact:

Willow Creek Association
P.O. Box 3188
Barrington, IL 60011-3188
Phone: 847-570-9812
Fax: 847-765-5046
www.willowcreek.com

Just Walk Across the Room Curriculum Kit

Simple Steps Pointing People to Faith

Bill Hybels with *Ashley Wiersma*

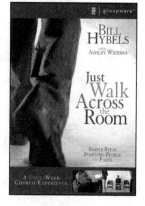

In *Just Walk Across the Room*, Bill Hybels brings personal evangelism into the twenty-first century with a natural and empowering approach modeled after Jesus himself. When Christ "walked" clear across the cosmos more than 2,000 years ago, he had no forced formulas and no memorized script; rather, he came armed only with an offer of redemption for people like us, many of whom were neck-deep in pain of their own making.

This dynamic four-week experience is designed to equip and inspire your entire church to participate in that same pattern of grace-giving by taking simple walks across rooms — leaving your circles of comfort and extending hands of care, compassion, and inclusiveness to people who might need a touch of God's love today.

Expanding on the principles set forth in Hybels' book of the same name, *Just Walk Across the Room* consists of three integrated components:

- Sermons, an implementation guide, and church promotional materials provided on CD-ROM to address the church as a whole
- Small group DVD and a participant's guide to enable people to work through the material in small, connected circles of community
- The book *Just Walk Across the Room* to allow participants to think through the concepts individually

Mixed Media Set: 978-0-310-27172-7

Pick up a copy at your favorite bookstore!

When the Game Is Over, It All Goes Back in the Box DVD

Six Sessions on Living Life in the Light of Eternity

John Ortberg with *Stephen* and *Amanda Sorenson*

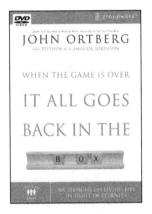

Using his humor and his genius for storytelling, John Ortberg helps you focus on the real rules of the game of life and how to set your priorities. *When the Game Is Over, It All Goes Back in the Box DVD* and participant's guide help explain how, left to our own devices, we tend to seek out worldly things, mistakenly thinking they will bring us fulfillment. But everything on Earth belongs to God. Everything we "own" is just on loan. And what pleases God is often 180 degrees from what we may think is important.

In the six sessions you will learn how to:

- Live passionately and boldly
- Learn how to be active players in the game that pleases God
- Find your true mission and offer your best
- Fill each square on the board with what matters most
- Seek the richness of being instead of the richness of having

You can't beat the house, notes Ortberg. We're playing our game of life on a giant board called a calendar. Time will always run out, so it's a good thing to live a life that delights your Creator. When everything goes back in the box, you'll have made what is temporary a servant to what is eternal, and you'll leave this life knowing you've achieved the only victory that matters.

This DVD includes a 32-page leader's guide and is designed to be used with the *When the Game Is Over, It All Goes Back in the Box* participant's guide, which is available separately.

DVD-ROM: 978-0-310-28247-1
Participant's Guide: 978-0-310-28246-4

Pick up a copy at your favorite bookstore!

The Case for Christ DVD

A Six-Session Investigation of the Evidence for Jesus

Lee Strobel and *Garry Poole*

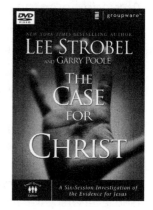

Is there credible evidence that Jesus of Nazareth really is the Son of God?

Retracing his own spiritual journey from atheism to faith, Lee Strobel, former legal editor of the *Chicago Tribune*, cross-examines several experts with doctorates from schools like Cambridge, Princeton, and Brandeis who are recognized authorities in their own fields.

Strobel challenges them with questions like:

- How reliable is the New Testament?
- Does evidence for Jesus exist outside the Bible?
- Is there any reason to believe the resurrection was an actual event?

Strobel's tough, point-blank questions make this six-session video study a captivating, fast-paced experience. But it's not fiction. It's a riveting quest for the truth about history's most compelling figure.

The six sessions include:

1. The Investigation of a Lifetime
2. Eyewitness Evidence
3. Evidence Outside the Bible
4. Analyzing Jesus
5. Evidence for the Resurrection
6. Reaching the Verdict

6 sessions; 1 DVD with leader's guide, 80 minutes (approximate).
The Case for Christ participant's guide is available separately.

DVD-ROM: 978-0-310-28280-8
Participant's Guide: 978-0-310-28282-2

The Case for a Creator DVD

A Six-Session Investigation of the Scientific Evidence That Points toward God

Lee Strobel and *Garry Poole*

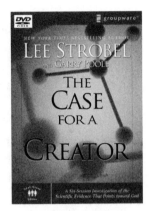

Former journalist and skeptic Lee Strobel has discovered something very interesting about science. Far from being the enemy of faith, science may now provide a solid foundation for believing in God.

Has science finally discovered God? Certainly new discoveries in such scientific disciplines as cosmology, cellular biology, astronomy, physics and DNA research are pointing to the incredible complexity of our universe, a complexity best explained by the existence of a Creator.

Written by Lee Strobel and Garry Poole, this six-session, 80-minute DVD curriculum comes with a companion participant's guide along with a leader's guide. The kit is based on Strobel's book and documentary *The Case for a Creator* and invites participants to encounter a diverse and impressive body of new scientific research that supports the belief in God. Weighty and complex evidence is delivered in a compelling conversational style.

The six sessions include:

1. Science and God
2. Doubts about Darwinism
3. The Evidence of Cosmology
4. The Fine-tuning of the Universe
5. The Evidence of Biochemistry
6. DNA and the Origin of Life

The Case for a Creator participant's guide is available separately.

DVD-ROM: 978-0-310-28283-9
Participant's Guide: 978-0-310-28285-3

The Case for Faith DVD

A Six-Session Investigation of the Toughest Objections to Christianity

Lee Strobel and *Garry Poole*

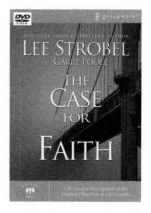

Doubt is familiar territory for Lee Strobel, the former atheist and award-winning author of books for skeptics and Christians. But he believes that faith and reason go hand in hand, and that Christianity is a defensible religion.

In this six-session video curriculum, Strobel uses his journalistic approach to explore the most common emotional obstacles to faith in Christ. These include the natural inclination to wrestle with faith and doubt, the troubling presence of evil and suffering in the world, and the exclusivity of the Christian gospel. They also include this compelling question: Can I doubt and be a Christian?

Through compelling video of personal stories and experts addressing these topics, combined with reflection and interaction, Christians and spiritual seekers will learn how to overcome these obstacles, deepen their spiritual convictions, and find new confidence that Christianity is a reasonable faith.

The Case for Faith participant's guide is available separately.

DVD-ROM: 978-0-310-24116-4
Participant's Guide: 978-0-310-24114-0

Pick up a copy at your favorite bookstore!

ReGroup™

Training Groups to Be Groups

Henry Cloud, Bill Donahue, and *John Townsend*

Whether you're a new or seasoned group leader, or whether your group is well-established or just getting started, the *ReGroup*™ small group DVD and participant's guide will lead you and your group together to a remarkable new closeness and effectiveness. Designed to foster healthy group interaction and facilitate maximum growth, this innovative approach equips both group leaders and members with essential skills and values for creating and sustaining truly life-changing small groups. Created by three group life experts, the two DVDs in this kit include:

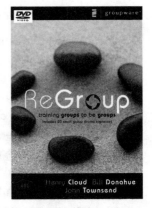

- Four sixty-minute sessions on the foundations of small groups that include teaching by the authors, creative segments, and activities and discussion time
- Thirteen five-minute coaching segments on topics such as active listening, personal sharing, giving and receiving feedback, prayer, calling out the best in others, and more

A participant's guide is sold separately.

DVD: 978-0-310-27783-5
Participant's Guide: 978-0-310-27785-9

Pick up a copy at your favorite bookstore!

No Perfect People Allowed
(with 4-Week Church Experience DVD)
Creating a Come as You Are Culture in the Church
John Burke

How do we live out the message of Jesus in today's ever-changing culture?

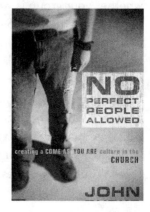

The church is facing its greatest challenge—and its greatest opportunity—in our postmodern, post-Christian world. God is drawing thousands of spiritually curious "imperfect people" to become his church—but how are we doing at welcoming them?

No Perfect People Allowed shows you how to deconstruct the five main barriers standing between emerging generations and your church by creating the right culture. From inspiring stories of real people once far from God, to practical ideas that can be applied by any local church, this book offers a refreshing vision of the potential and power of the body of Christ to transform lives today.

> "We now are living in a post-Christian America—and that means we must be rethinking ministry through a missionary mindset. What makes this book both unique and extremely helpful is that it is filled with real-life stories of post-Christian people becoming followers of Jesus—not just statistics or data about them."
>
> Dan Kimball, Author, *The Emerging Church*

> "... John's 'get it' factor with people, lost or found, is something to behold! Reading this book filled me with optimism regarding the next generation of pastors and faith communities ... "
>
> Bill Hybels, Senior Pastor, Willow Creek Community Church

> "*No Perfect People Allowed* is a timely and necessary word for church leaders in a post-Christian culture. John Burke serves up quite a tasty meal full of the rich nutrients that will strengthen the body of Christ."
>
> Randy Frazee, Senior Minister, Oak Hills Church; Author, *The Connecting Church* and *Making Room for Life*

Hardcover, Jacketed: 978-0-310-27807-8

Share Your Thoughts

With the Author: Your comments will be forwarded to the author when you send them to *zauthor@zondervan.com*.

With Zondervan: Submit your review of this book by writing to *zreview@zondervan.com*.

Free Online Resources at
www.zondervan.com/hello

 Zondervan AuthorTracker: Be notified whenever your favorite authors publish new books, go on tour, or post an update about what's happening in their lives.

 Daily Bible Verses and Devotions: Enrich your life with daily Bible verses or devotions that help you start every morning focused on God.

 Free Email Publications: Sign up for newsletters on fiction, Christian living, church ministry, parenting, and more.

 Zondervan Bible Search: Find and compare Bible passages in a variety of translations at www.zondervanbiblesearch.com.

 Other Benefits: Register yourself to receive online benefits like coupons and special offers, or to participate in research.